Men, Beware of a Woman If…

By B. Nathaniel Smith

Men, Beware of a Woman If…
By B. Nathaniel Smith

Printed in the United States of America

ISBN 978-1-365-76389-2

TABLE OF CONTENTS

INTRODUCTION

Men Beware of a Woman If…

Here we go again. Not another one. Are you serious? Is this another book about relationships? Don't we already have enough books about relationships and the male and female genders? Who is going to read this book when there are so many others sitting unread? We already know that men and women seem to hail from completely different points of view. Do we really need to hear another interpretation of how to interact with one another? Is this book about how we are to communicate and connect with one another, or how our differences make us who we are as people? Do we really need THIS book?

Yes, this is another book about relationships, both platonic and intimate. Yes, this book is serious in its attempt to convey the reality of how men and women are different—but it is also meant to convey how these differences, if understood, can make for better social and behavioral interactions. I won't insult your intelligence with mediocre and trivial monologues of the X and Y chromosomal differences. However, I will stimulate your brain cells and your emotional wherewithal to consider, if nothing more, how three Female Types can change a man's entire perception of himself and his perspective on life in general. There are learned behaviors and then there are genetic behaviors that are intrinsic, and people are prone to both.

This book will be unlike any book you have ever read. It's direct, blatant, honest, unapologetic, and will definitely force you to identify with one, if not all of the Female Types mentioned. I kept the book short, as most men do not like to read and most women would like men to say what they feel. Therefore, I have attempted to meet the needs of both genders in this respect.

Furthermore, this book unveils what women think and feel, and what men wish they knew about women but were too afraid to ask. This book could be called a "man's quick reference guide to Female Types," because it introduces you to three major categories of females that are dominant in our society: Tulip, Lily, and Daffodil. Each of these types is completely different in character, persona, and behavioral responses that influence how they interact with men. As you read this book, be open, and be willing to make changes, and, if you are a woman, do not be afraid to acknowledge the type of female you are.

Regardless of where you find yourself in this book, if you are not going to deal with who you are as a person, then you will never, ever understand the basis of what this book represents. You are supposed to be offended, challenged, and caught off guard emotionally. You are supposed to think retrospectively on your past, what you are experiencing in your present, and what you want your future to become. You should want to assess your current lifestyle and the types of friends, lovers, associates, and family members with whom you interact. It's very important to create boundaries, establish some measure of discipline in your decision-making process, and decide what's best for you. In other words, you must make some decisions!

Yes, this is a "man's quick reference guide to Female Types," but it's also a "female's guide to Female Types." Females should read this book and determine which "type" they are. Once this has been determined, you will know how and why you have a particular kind of impact and influence on others. Men, after reading this book you should be able to determine and identify each Female Type from across the room…from across the parking lot…in a grocery store…at a social event…at their family reunion…in their neighborhood…in their bedroom! I can guarantee you one thing—whether you are a female who is reading this or a male who is skimming through each chapter, you will never look at females or relationships the same.

FEMALE TYPES

As you read this book, there are key words, phrases, and even concepts that will resonate from each page and chapter of this book. Your ability to become familiar with the "characteristics" and "identities" of each Female Type is crucial. This section will provide you with a brief but concise "word-match" related to each Female Type. Learn them well…you will need to know them moving forward!

Tulip

Nurturer
Older
Wiser
Experienced
Non-judgmental
Confident

Established
Secure
Advocate
Private
Discreet
Secretive

Lily

Talented
Dependable
Trustworthy
Gullible
Great Listener

Classy
Focused
Socially Adept
Witty

Daffodil

Independent
Focused
Secure/Insecure
Opinionated
Controlling
Manipulative
Holds Grudges

Narcissistic
Deceptive
Cunning
Poisonous
Territorial
Gossips
Aggressive

Be willing to refer to this section often as you continue reading through this book. You will find that you could probably come up with quite a few additional words that are not listed in my tables. Be creative…be honest!

CHAPTER 1: SKIN DEEP: REVISITED

In my previous book, *5 Ways to Affirm a Man*, I dedicated Chapter 1 to the concept of Skin Deep. I'm going to include a large portion of that discussion here, to prepare the reader for their relationship-building opportunity with the Female Types. If this is your first time reading this passage, take note. If you read my first book, then this will serve as a recap for you.

If you were to research dermatology, you will learn that the skin has layers that mend by replacing damaged or old layers on a daily basis. In addition, the skin has multiple layers called the Epidermis, Dermis, and the Subcutaneous. Each layer functions differently but works together as one organ. The epidermis is the outermost layer of the skin, and it contains five layers called the stratum basal, stratum spinosum, stratum granulosom, stratum licidum, and stratum corneum. The dermis is the middle layer and noted for its stretching ability due to its composition of collagen and elastin fibers. In this middle layer, the pain and touch receptors carry impulses to the brain. Finally, the subcutaneous is the bottom layer and is a source of energy and a major conservation source of heat.

The discussion of skin layers is important to your ability to understand the impact that women possess on men. What do I mean by that? Glad you asked that question. As you read through this book and, hopefully, gain a better understanding of the various Female Types (Tulip, Lily, and Daffodil), it is my desire for you to understand that any man can be hurt emotionally, physically, spiritually, and psychologically by a woman. Oftentimes, the results are not obvious until the impact is long over. By that time, the impact could have been extremely detrimental and possibly un-repairable, or it could be exactly what's needed to strengthen a relationship, be it platonic or intimate.

Because of numerous media images, propaganda, and music videos that exploit women negatively, many images of women are shown in a tainted, compromising, and extremely questionable platform. Allow me to take this brief time to share with you how there is a direct correlation between skin layers and the physical, emotional, and psychological state of a woman. I will seek to explain the power of a woman and what the results can be when that impact is **Skin Deep** and the **Correlative** result is exemplified via the physical, emotional, and psychological state of a woman.

CORRELATIVE

I can't even begin this section until I have taken the time to include some very simple yet profound definitions that will completely impact your understanding of the Female Types. Please take a moment to review the following terms. I can assure you that if they had not previously been a part of your vocabulary, after reading through this section you will want to pause, reflect, sigh, and even chuckle at its relevance to your life. Read on!

> "Correlative (adjective). 1. Related; corresponding. 2. Indicating a reciprocal or complementary relationship."[1]
>
> "Complementary (adjective). 1. Forming or serving as a complement; completing. 2. Supplying mutual needs or lacks."[2]
>
> "Complimentary (adjective). 1. Expressing, using, or resembling a compliment."[3]
>
> "Compliment (noun). 1. An expression of praise, admiration, or congratulation."[4]

The correlation of skin layers (Dermis, Epidermis, and Subcutaneous) is directly related to the physical, emotional, and psychological state of the Female Types (Tulip, Lily, and Daffodil).

---

[1] The American Heritage Dictionary. 2nd ed. Boston, MA: Houghton Mifflin Company, 1985.
[2] Ibid., i.
[3] Ibid., i.
[4] Ibid., i.

The schematic depiction below should add visual clarity:

FEMALE TYPE	SKIN LAYER	STATE OF BEING
Tulip	Dermis (Middle)	Physical
Lily	Epidermis (Top)	Emotional
Daffodil	Subcutaneous (Bottom)	Psychological

As a reminder, the skin layers can easily be remembered as Dermis (middle layer), Epidermis (top layer), and the Subcutaneous (deepest layer). Now that we have completed our basic biological understanding of the skin, let's venture into the specific state of being of each of the Female Types.

TULIP (Dermis/Physical)

The Dermis is the middle layer and noted for its stretching ability due to its composition of collagen (*constituent of bone, cartilage, and connective tissue)* and elastin fibers. In other words, the Dermis is what keeps things connected…flexible…unbreakable! The Female Type best suited for this skin layer is Tulip. Her *State of Being* is *Physical*. That means she is involved, connected, and willing to add support and strength to any given situation. Her age, experience, and knowledge are what immediately distinguishes her from the other two Female Types. Tulip has seen life in action. The other Female Types don't have the same life experiences upon which to reflect. Tulip has endured through memorable protests, monumental legislation, and remarkable movements in education reform, social phenomena, and environmental improvements.

Every man should have the ability to be connected to a Tulip. She understands what it means to adapt to her ever-changing surroundings and yet maintain the essence of her being. She is a woman with a rich history, uncompromising standard, and can convey thought and understanding without the use of a textbook, higher level degree, or a six-figure salary, if need be. Though it matters to be educationally astute and striving towards the American dream of home ownership, family, finances, and the sort, Tulip is content whether she resides in the backwoods of the smallest country town with its red dirt signature or if she was the president of her own company in the bastion of corporate America. Adaptation is her emblem. Oftentimes, she doesn't say much because she is an observer. She knows how to internalize situations to the point where her wisdom becomes even more valuable. She is a woman of few words because she learned a long time ago that "brevity is the soul of wit." In other words, she knows much but says little. So she observes, mentally categorizes what she sees, and waits until the appropriate time to add value to others.

Tulip is the backbone of a marriage. She is the stabilizer of the children. She is the pillar for her husband. She is the reassuring voice that dries up the tears of a hurting child. She is the soothing calm to a man who has been battered, abused, and disrespected by life itself. She is the protector of her family. She is involved, physical, and the dermis for her community. She is all of these things, yet she is flawed...she is mortal...she has influence...she has positively and negatively affected the life of a man. How could she not, for she is a woman. Be mindful, even the Dermis can be stretched to the point of breaking.

LILY (Epidermis/Emotional)

The Epidermis is the top layer of the skin, which is supported by five underlying layers. For sake of this discussion, our focus will be primarily on the Epidermis itself. The Epidermis is what one can visually see with the naked eye. It is what captivates or repels us. It is what we can make a judgment about or that which we can compliment accordingly. It's elusive, or at least it can be most of the time. On the other hand, it's so realistic that we wrestle internally to assure ourselves that what we see is truly, what is.

The Female Type that undoubtedly embodies this skin layer is Lily. Her S*tate of Being* is *Emotional.* Lily is vulnerable. She is exposed. She is subjected to and reactive to the climate, the seasons, and human touch. She is affected by what she sees, hears, and feels. She is secure yet insecure. She is stable yet unstable. She is strong yet susceptible to the weaknesses of others, which becomes a weakness of her own. She is the kind of woman who begins with the right intentions and motives but is often taken advantage of and left trying to put her life back together. She loves quickly and easily. She falls hard and fast. She recovers quickly but is visibly bruised in the process. She trusts too easily. She forgives much too quickly. She is often in the same detrimental situation repeatedly. Partially because she believes in people and she believes in love. Partially because she is immature in some places and broken in other places. She may seek attention to cover her inadequacies. She may shy away or appear to be introverted for fear of being hurt again. Yet, she is so trusting that it is sometimes hard for her to see the truth through the fallacies of her relationships. And with all of this, she is inviting, comforting, and non-threatening.

Lily has an air of class coupled with a solid education. She is an amazing listener and can handle her own in any professional environment. She is consistent, predictable, and aware of what others expect from her. She is her own personal critic, and most of the time she is very hard on herself. She would rather forgive others for what they have done to her than to forgive herself for having been in that situation at all. Her signature stamp on the lives of others is that she is a giver. She is loving, believes in love, and will always search for love—regardless of how much it may hurt when she doesn't find it in those from whom she expects it. She has many childhood secrets and memorable moments of regret, loss, and abandonment. Many of those feelings have never been dealt with, even though she is now a woman who may have a husband, children, and employees that depend upon her. She can be an over-achiever, the top of her class or the top performer in her career. Yet, she is lonely, afraid, and on many isolated occasions, she has contemplated suicide…oftentimes when she was at the height of her career or at times when she seemed happiest.

Lily is the Female Type that appears strong, focused, and secure. She is the marrying type and would be committed and supportive of her mate. She is the most damaged of all the Female Types but is the one who holds the most potential for leaving the most impressionable mark upon any Male Type. It is very important not to take for granted the virtue of a Lily. Remember, she is correlative to the Epidermis, the most vulnerable, exposed, and least protected skin layer. In other words, there are more Lily's prevalent than there are Tulips or Daffodils. Yet, because of Lily's susceptibility to bruising, she is also the Female Type who is most prone to transitioning from a Lily into a Daffodil. And when that occurs, it's no longer emotional for her—she becomes vindictive, plotting, and calculating. She creates multiple walls to protect her heart, all the while going into survival and attack mode.

DAFFODIL (Subcutaneous/Psychological)

The Subcutaneous level of the skin layers is the deepest, lowest, and hardest to reach layer. It is the least exposed, hardest to injure, and as it is the bottom layer, it is a source of energy and a major conservation source of heat. The Female Type that embodies this skin layer is Daffodil. Her *State of Being* is *Psychological.* Daffodil has the uncanny ability to influence the mind and the emotions of any man. She is skilled in reasoning, emotional foreplay, and suggestive thought. She can be misleading, hard to comprehend, and is known for her ability to play games with your mind. She can be spiteful, deceiving, disruptive, abrasive, and brash. She can be subtle yet poisonous as a viper. She can be as silent and deadly as a vapor or as obtrusive and obstructive as a heart attack. She is always opinionated, untrusting, known for gossiping, and very controlling. Yet, she is independent, intelligent, street smart, and is the originator of the ability to disguise her intent by "masking" herself in any given situation.

Daffodil has learned to use the opportunities of this world to advance and sustain her selfish motives. She will use and corrupt family members, her children, her husband, her friends, and even her employees, if need be. She is very smart in the fact that she has contemplated every angle of her escape, regardless of what controversy she may be embroiled in. Part of her survival technique is that she has some hidden "dirt" on everyone around her. She does not play fair and will always—and I mean always—have a trump card. The problem is, she may play it too soon and could potentially end up hurting others who would not normally have been involved at all.

To understand Daffodil is to understand the role of the female Black Widow spider and that of the female Praying Mantis. The female Black Widow spider is physically bigger in size than the male, and she is known for being highly venomous and for eating the male after copulation. She is beautiful, and because of the red markings under her abdomen that has been known to resemble an hourglass, she is visually captivating and intriguing. The female Black Widow spider is well known for biting humans, whereas the males very rarely bite humans at all. This would denote a higher level of aggressive tendency on the part of the female and also a territorial power struggle. She rarely, if ever, leaves her web because that's her base. In other words, she expects that you will come to her and meet her on her own turf. She will lure you in and before you know it, she has you smitten and bitten!

Now, in my research, I found out that when a female Black Widow spider bites you, you normally would not know it. It's not until the symptoms of the venom become prevalent that you know you have been bitten. More specifically, when bitten, the results of a bite can be soreness all over your body; pain in areas of your being that can impact your vision and your thinking. There may be sweating, as if your pores have been opened and a flood is ensuing. But most of all, you will be paralyzed. And it's not until you are paralyzed that she moves in for the actual kill. She is patient, methodical, and completely unresponsive to how you may be feeling. She will wait…and wait…and wait until the appropriate time, and then she destroys you. Your mind, body, and soul are completely devastated by her. You will become nothing more than a resource for her. Without anti-venom, death becomes you—not a physical death but the death of your manhood, your instinct, and your ability to rationalize and make decisions.

Men, if you are reading this section on Daffodil, pay very close attention to all of the key words in this section. I would even encourage you to circle them, highlight them, or put a line under them. You will undoubtedly see a correlation between the words used in this section and the Daffodil Female Type you have encountered. Here is an interesting thought: regardless of your ethnicity, race, culture, or even socio-economic status, a Daffodil is a Daffodil is a Daffodil. She comes in all colors, can be of any race, possess any physical stature, and even have her own personal style. You need to understand, her looks won't be the demarcation in the sand that distinguishes her from the other Female Types. You won't be able to just look at her and say, oh that's a Daffodil. It's not until you engage her or you become engaged by her. It's not until you have been captivated by her that you realize you have been infected and affected by her. More to come on that in later chapters.

Now, allow me to go back to our discussion on insects. In contrast, the female Praying Mantis doesn't inject her mate with venom or wait until there is a paralyzed state. She immediately goes for taking off his head. Literally! The female Praying Mantis is also physically larger than the males, with a noticeably wider abdomen. She is undoubtedly a carnivore. Furthermore, cannibalism among this species has been observed and noted when the female is hungry. After mating, if the male does not fly away or move rather quickly away from the vicinity of the female, she will devour him by taking off his head first, consuming it, and then making her way through the rest of his body until she is satisfied or full—whichever comes first.

Self-preservation is Daffodil's sole purpose, and that may come at the sacrifice of her male counterpart—or of other males, if necessary—in order to sustain her longevity. The irony is that many men are attracted to a Daffodil. Daffodils possess a free-spirited autonomy that immediately comes through via their character. They are perceived as being independent and carefree. They can come across as flirty and mysterious, which immediately sparks the interest of a man. Anything a man can't explain or control, he tries to explore and conquer. And Daffodil is the Female Type that is well known for having many explorers become extinct. It could be her looks, it could be her energy/vibe, or it could just be the "pheromones" that she emits in order to attract a male. Regardless, any man who has encountered a Daffodil in his life and has lived to tell the tale will definitely have some internal wounds to show for it. But why wouldn't he? Her trademark is her venom or her damage to your head (mind)…and it always leaves a lasting impression on her prey!

Psychologically, any man who has spent even a small amount of time with a Daffodil is psychologically impacted. His thinking, his emotions, and even his reactions are paralyzed to some extent, and without therapy and an antidote, he will continue to infect others along his life because the venom of Daffodil will remain in his veins. Without an antidote, she will eventually drain him of his energy and his will, reducing him to nothing but a mere skeleton of a man. Beware of her bite. Most never know they have been bitten until it's already too late and she has gotten **Skin Deep!**

REGENERATION: THE WOLVERINE EFFECT

Our physical bodies are able to recover from many types of injuries. Normally, regeneration occurs with time, rest, and some level of exercise. Sometimes, our healing or regeneration process can be quick and not as painful, depending upon the type of damage done. For example, a cut on the arm from a small tree branch or a scraped knee from falling down on the cement may not take as long to heal compared to that of a broken arm or fractured pelvic bone from a car accident. Both examples denote some pain and recovery time but both examples have significantly different pain levels and recovery periods associated with them. Healing is a process but recovery is a completely different concept altogether. One can heal from a wound, but mentally, one may never recover.

As a child, I can recollect a childhood chant that went something like this: "Sticks and stones may break my bones but names will never hurt me." At that time, children would use this chant to defend off other children who would call them names or who would bully them. As an adult, the reality is that one can heal from broken bones caused by sticks and stones but the recovery process for being called names and from being bullied may be ongoing. That's why this segment is known as **The Wolverine Effect!**

Wolverine is a character in the *X-Men* movie series known for having long, metallic claws that extend from in between his fingers when he is angered or threatened. What's amazing about him is that if injured, regardless of how severe the wound, he can heal sometimes within seconds of the injury being inflicted. So in essence, it is very difficult, if not impossible, to kill him. But if you were to watch any of the *X-Men* movies, you will come to find that as strong as Wolverine is, and as tough as he presents himself to be as a man, he is consistently haunted by his past and unable to fully recover from it. There are a host of questions and emotions that he encounters as he considers whether or not he is a villain and wants to do his own thing or if he is a superhero defending the cause of all mutants. He can recover from his physical wounds, but he can't recover the life that was taken from him at an early age.

As an adolescent, he was by birth a mutant. At that time, his claws were bonelike in nature and not metallic. It wasn't until he became an adult that he had a surgical procedure occur wherein his entire skeletal frame was altered by a metallic compound, which made him nearly indestructible. And herein lies the correlation of Wolverine to that of the Female Types. Women are regenerators by nature. They can heal from rejection. They can heal from abuse. They can heal from damage that's been done to their emotions. They can teach children and other women how to endure and heal. They are the epitome of reproduction for our nation, and they have endured so much foolishness from men that they can easily be compared to the regenerative ability of Wolverine.

A woman can easily reinvent herself. She can change her hair, her style of dress, her mannerisms, and even her attitude—sometimes simultaneously! Her regenerative power is so amazingly innate that she can even change a man into who she wants him to become because of her "influential power." Women have two notable "influential powers" or abilities to which every man is subject. They have the power of influence itself and they have the power of love. Both can be a detriment or benefit depending upon how they are used. I have heard it said that a woman is closest to death when giving birth to a child. If this is indeed true, then their ability to regenerate their body during and after childbirth is an amazing and completely profound biological and spiritual feat.

What's even more amazing is the length of time that it can take a man to recover from being wounded by a female. Men are not designed as women are. If men could give birth, they probably would not be able to endure the first couple of months of the pregnancy due to the physical and hormonal changes that they will encounter. I won't even talk about the birthing time, labor, pain, and delivery. I have heard tales of 200-pound men who lift weights and can handle all manner of physical labor, faint at the sight of blood or at the birth of a baby. The women can endure it, but it's the men who are weakened just by being in the same room.

Women, hear me. You have the power to weaken a man when you touch his heart and his mind. If you negatively impact those two vital organs, he will be able to regenerate, but he will not fully recover without therapy. Men, use this section of the book to realize that women have power, know how to use it, and sometimes it may result in serious injury to you. Men, even when damaged, we may appear to have regenerated externally but we recover significantly slower than women.

In dealing with a Tulip, our regeneration and recovery time frame are much quicker because her initial intent is not to harm. It's when she has exhausted all efforts to be cordial and humanistic that her impact is felt more substantially. In dealing with a Lily, our emotions take a much longer time to deal with, as we would have worked to gain her trust and heart so we have put much more effort into connecting with her. So when we are hurt by her, we feel it much deeper and it resonates much longer than that of a Tulip. Time, relocation, and a change of habits will help you in your regeneration process, though your internal recovery will require more time.

In dealing with a Daffodil, the recovery and regeneration process is confusing. We think we are healed until we begin to meet and interact with other women with similar personality types of a Daffodil. We get in a rut and begin to repeat the same lifestyle over and over again. We begin confusing arguments and ignoring one another for love and affection or for care and concern. We don't realize we have not healed until we become overly sensitive and defensive at the same time. We don't realize we have not recovered from the last Daffodil encounter until we begin to reference our last relationship (our past) while dealing with issues in our current relationship (present). We begin to draw comparisons of what we liked in our past to what we don't like in our present. This in turn inadvertently impacts our future. We have not regenerated nor have we recovered. What begins to happen is a layer of hurt, rejection, fear, and a feeling of inadequacy builds within us and our thinking is off. We become suspicious of every woman who crosses our path. If we are not careful, we may end up bitter, alone, and disrespectful of women because we have not taken the time to regenerate our emotions and allow our hearts and minds to recover from a bad encounter with a Daffodil.

Men listen, you can have The Wolverine Effect, but it usually occurs with the help of a particular Female Type, and the healing process can take a long time. In order to recover, you will have to learn to avoid dealing with a Daffodil…if you can! You will have to realize that Tulip is like a mother—but she is not *your* mother. Be willing to draw the line.

Don't be so quick to fall for a Lily just because she is Lily. Remember, she may be who you desire to be with, but because of her past, she will have a lot of baggage with her. Unless you are willing to unpack each "luggage set" bag by bag and item by item, and unless you are willing to invest a significant amount of patience and recovery time, move very slowly with this Female Type. She is fragile in many areas of her private life, but remember, you won't see that initially—you would only see her Epidermis! Don't be fooled!

CHAPTER 2: TULIP

The most distinguished of all of the Female Types is Tulip. The key and only reason for such a denotation is the fact that she has time and experience as her resume. Tulip is normally an older woman who has seen men come and go. She has witnessed hurt, pain, rejection, and loss. She has endured beyond separations, break ups, restraining orders, and adultery. She is the kind of woman who would tell you the truth about a man just by looking at him. Oftentimes she is ninety-eight percent correct. Other times, she can be biased and opinionated—especially when you didn't ask for it. Her ability to use her experience as a panacea for every relationship discussion she has is a fault that she doesn't notice. She is quick to tell you a story about something that occurred in her past or about something that she heard happen to someone else. She never tires of a good story, and the more you hear it, the more it may become an embellished myth than honest truth. Yet her overall intentions are pure, and she is intrinsically concerned about others. Her mothering nature shines through effortlessly. She will give you her last just to ensure that you are not lacking. But she will more than likely remind you of it every single conversation you have with her.

Most men say that they want a woman who is similar to their mother…but in Tulip's case, you may be getting more than what you bargained for. Once you are emotionally connected to this Female Type, it's hard to then create the boundaries that should have been created from the genesis. Tulip can sometimes be the smothering, fixing your clothes in public, wiping food off your top lip kind of a woman. She can sometimes be the calling too much, wondering where you are every second, when will you be coming back kind of a woman. Because she is concerned, caring, and cohesive, it's hard to tell her to back off or give you some space. But you have to. If you do not, you will then become as her child and not as her mate. And that's always a problem for a man to be relegated to a child status when he wants to be recognized as a man. Could that be the reason why so many women meet men who act like children? Could this be because of their interaction with a Tulip, and so they never matured and grew up because they didn't have to? Or could this speak to Tulip's insecurity of not wanting to be alone or lonely and of not wanting to feel like she can't contribute to another? This is a perfect time to explore how "concerned" Tulip can be and what happens when that concern becomes overbearing for her mate.

CONCERNED

If I were coming from a spiritual perspective, then Tulip would be the "priestess" of her household. She is concerned about all that goes on around her. She is a humanitarian who believes in her people, her community, her relationships, and the perceptions of others. She can be overly spiritual and religious, or she can have an appearance of being such, though she may not totally subscribe to it personally. She has to be seen as the one who is trying to make it better for all others. Sometimes, she will do this at a substantial sacrifice to her finances, time, and energy. She can be the strong advocate on her block or she could be the soft speaking yet sharp-tongued individual in her family. She has a history of handling loss well because she has been able to rebound past it and the longer she lives the easier it becomes for her. Many times, she won't let you know exactly what she is thinking or what's going on in her life because she has such a strong image to uphold—even if that image is for her own personal gain.

Men who meet Tulip are immediately comforted by the fact that she is easy going and accepting of most of their issues and flaws without reminding them of those issues or flaws. Men find it easy to communicate with Tulip because she is an amazing listener. What men don't realize until much later is that she listens for her own gain, so that she will have leverage if ever needed in the future. Most of the time her concern for you is genuine because there is always a benefit in it for her…even if she has to wait a while until it comes forth. She will wait and bide her time accordingly. Tulip realizes that this is a tough world and that every stray dog eventually has to come home. So she will allow you to run the streets, and still keep the bed warm for you. She will allow you to come in with another woman's scent on you, run your shower, fix your dinner (supper, depending on who is reading this), and even hand you the remote control when you are ready for it. She enjoys your company, and though she can be alright if she were alone, she would prefer not to be alone. So she endures. She is well known for showing you she loves you by the overshadowing reach of her concern for you. Many times, she will speak on your behalf, offer her opinion in place of yours, and make decisions for you without regard to waiting for your reply. She is without question your biggest advocate and will back you up and protect you even when you are completely wrong.

With everything that Tulip is and can be, she is very private and is well known for keeping secrets. She will continually press you for information about you and your life, all the while keeping her feelings very close to her bosom. She is so skilled in studying and understanding men that she forgets that studying without application is only information. She chooses her words carefully so as not to offend and is accepting of your behaviors when most women would have left a long time ago. But that's what makes her a Tulip. She is patient, enduring, and cautious. She is secretive yet passionate about the things that concern you. She will always struggle with understanding the difference in being too overbearing and that of being loving. To her, it means the same thing. To a man, it's intrusive and has its limits. Most men take for granted that women know when they are being too overbearing, and that's a common mistake that men use to blame women. It's the responsibility of the man to communicate when he is feeling smothered by Tulip—not hers to know when to pull back. But once it is communicated, why is it that Tulip has a problem with pulling back? It's because of her caring and protective nature. And that may be the very thing that destroys her relationships with others.

CARING

Tulip understands that most men want a woman who is similar to their mother in some respects, which is why she takes great care in ensuring that the things she does will remind her mate of that "at home" nurturing feeling. For example, a smart Tulip will do certain things in order to keep her man interested and around. She will listen to you talk about things from your childhood or your past, and she will invariably incorporate those things into your relationship.

I am reminded of a story about a Tulip who recalled her man (let's call him Volos) telling her that, as a child, he enjoyed when his mother would make him warm milk with cinnamon when he wasn't feeling well. Once, on a cold winter evening, Volos returned home from a long day at work. When he got in and had changed his attire, he mentioned that he was feeling a little ill and wanted to just lie down and rest. Not even fifteen minutes later, Tulip walked into the bedroom with a mug of hot milk with cinnamon. Completely caught off guard, Volos accepted her offer without question because of two key reasons: he had a need, and she was able to meet it! Those are very important reasons why a man won't outright reject a Tulip and also why he finds it hard to pull away from her when he is overwhelmed by her. She knows how to meet his need, and he knows she is available. That can't be said of any other Female Type like it can be said of Tulip. She is available, and she has learned how to meet his need. Another woman can be willing and able, but there is no other woman who exemplifies and epitomizes the caring and nurturing way of a Tulip.

This, in turn, makes the man co-dependent upon Tulip, which is why you find many older women (the term cougar is not applicable) with much younger men. Even if men don't say it, they like to feel safe and protected as well. Many times, society denotes that a man should provide these comforts for a woman, but in a relationship, both individuals should provide an element of safety and protection for one another. How else would you protect the longevity of the relationship if the both of you are not on guard? A man cannot expect a woman to meet his every need and not lose some sense of control of his emotions to her.

Tulips get solace out of knowing that they have met the needs of their man. It drives them to do it more frequently, even at their own detriment sometimes. Yet, Tulips are smart. They realize that they only have a certain window of opportunity to infiltrate a man's heart, so they begin almost immediately trying to find out about their childhood, their relationship with their mother and aunts, and also their interaction with their father. Tulips are intuitive and smart. They have learned how to keep a man coming back, and back, and back again. The problem for the man may be when is enough, enough?

COHESIVE

Tulip, the non-judgmental, confident, established, and secure Female Type is very focused. In other words, Tulip is the most cohesive Female Type there is. To clarify, I don't mean perfect and the one who has it all figured out. I do mean she is a great support, comfort, and security measure for any insecure man. Most insecure men would flock to a Tulip because she has the resources he may be lacking, and she is more open to sharing her resources with him without making him feel as if he is less than a man. He can be himself around her without fear of her running and telling her girlfriends or her family members. He can trust that she would keep whatever he divulged to her in private.

Because she is pretty well established, she has created a comfort zone into which he can run and find rest. She is constantly striving to do the right thing, the right way, all the time. This in turn makes her appear to be perfect, and sometimes she may forget that she has imperfections. See, she knows the things about her that are great—or are on the way to being great. She doesn't know the things about her that she needs to work on, and this is where the friction comes in to play.

Many times, a man will leave a Tulip for fear of losing his element of self-control and identity. Many times, a Tulip would have no knowledge as to why he left. She met his need, she was available, she let him do what he wanted to do—she is at a loss for understanding. What a Tulip fails to realize is that she is his mate, not his mother. She didn't give birth to him. She didn't walk with him through his terrible twos. She didn't potty train him. She didn't help him with his homework. She didn't put the peroxide on the cut he received from falling off his bike. She didn't explain to him about the birds and bees and educate him about what it means to go through puberty. She didn't help him with his first kiss, and she wasn't there when he graduated or dropped out (whichever is applicable) from high school. All of these things are what a mother is normally charged with doing…not a mate. So when a Tulip takes on the position of being a mother instead of being a mate, it not only confuses a man but it is also nostalgic to him.

Tulip, don't be a mother, be a mate. Know your boundaries. Know your limitations. Stop impersonating his mother and be the mate that he needs you to be. Be his woman… allow him to stand on his own two feet. Stop buckling him in the car seat and by all means, remove the high chair into which you keep putting him. He shouldn't need a bib at this point in his development. Grow up, Tulip. You would think that as old and mature as you are, you would know better. But that's the problem; you have not had anyone tell you directly. Let the man be the man. You be his woman. And if all else fails, you just be the mature woman that time and experience has called you to be without the confusion of what your real role should be. Not his mother…but his mate!

CHAPTER 3: LILY

It is my hope that as you read each chapter in this book, you are realizing something more about who it is that you are as a woman. If you are a man reading this book, I hope that you are realizing something more about the types of relationships to which you are exposed or are enduring at this present time. One can't expect positive change to occur in one's life without some serious acknowledgement of who you are, where you are, and where you want to be in life. It sometimes takes a very strong hand to push us in front of the mirror of reality and say "Look at yourself, man…look at yourself, woman…you are not who you want to be and you are not who you should be."

We need to make change, and sometimes that change must be drastic. At other times, that change may be much slower and methodical in its purpose. Regardless of where you are, if you know you want to have a much more stable, solid, and secure relationship, then make the change today. Don't wait, don't procrastinate, and don't second-guess yourself. Make the change immediately. If you don't have peace in your soul about your relationship, then you won't ever be able to give a piece of your heart to your mate.

That's where Lily resides. She is at the crossroads of peace in her soul and determining how to give a piece of her heart to the right man. There is a constant wrestling that occurs in her heart and in her mind. Should she continue to be open and vulnerable, or should she be guarded and non-trusting? She has been open and vulnerable only to be taken advantage of and betrayed. She has been guarded and non-trusting, only to lose the one man she knew she needed but didn't know how to keep. When he made attempts to get close, she rejected him out of fear of past rejections…none of which he caused her. And now she compares every man to him, as none of the new men she has met truly measures up. Yet, she tries. On the outside, everyone sees her confidence. On the inside, no one sees her fears. Can she recover?

CONFIDENT

Lily is always confident that she can recover from any situation. She is just getting tired of continually having to recover. She is the type of a woman who seems always to have it together. She is focused, striving hard to do well for herself, and always seems to have been dealt a very rough hand as it relates to life. As soon as she makes two steps ahead, here comes a man and she finds herself three steps back. Her girlfriends continually ask her why she keeps meeting the same types of men, and she really doesn't know how to answer them other than to say, "I wasn't ready for anything serious." But we all know that's not the truth, and it's unfortunate that Lily would have to deceive her friends in an effort to conceal her tendency to fall in love too fast. She can't bear to hear her girlfriends berate her for making another foolish mistake—the same foolish mistake that she has made so many times before. She would rather they think of her as the confident, secure, and upwardly mobile woman that they could all depend upon. Yet inside, she is crying out for a male counterpart upon whom she can depend.

See, for Lily, keeping busy and staying preoccupied are what helps her maintain her consistency and a sense of security. It's when she is distracted by men that she loses herself, and her world begins to crumble from the inside out. She has asked herself time and time again, *"What am I doing wrong and what is wrong with me?"* She has never gotten an answer to those questions. If you are a Lily, or you are a female and you know a Lily, don't be too hard on yourself and don't be too hard on her. She really does desire to have a meaningful, lasting, and loving relationship. She has every intention of being committed, and she definitely wants to be able to give herself wholly to someone. Her fault is that she is the one standing in the way of her ultimate happiness—and getting that person out of the way is fully in her own hands. Until Lily is willing to deal with her past hurts and issues, she will be the enemy of her own state of being. So she will continue to excel outwardly. She will continue to say the right things, smile the correct way, and mask her true feelings and sentiment…all to fit in and be accepted. In her realm, being nice and keeping unnecessary attention off of her is what makes her complete. At least, that's what she thinks.

COMPLETE

Of all the Female Types, Lily has the ability to convey her sincerity the best. Now, that's not to say that the other Female Types are less than capable of displaying theirs on some level, but sincerity comes naturally for Lily. Her ability to display her sincerity signifies a level of completeness or wholeness for her. Every man looks for a woman who could add value to him. Many men may say that they don't want to settle down, and that they just want to be friends, but that's not entirely true. Sure, there are some single men who enjoy their independence and liberty to go and do as they please without having to give an account for their whereabouts. But most men would love to be able to have that one woman who understands them and who wants them around as much as they want her to be around. But because of pride, most men miss out on the opportunity to meet Lily where she is and allow her completeness of being to echo his completeness of being, thereby adding value to both of their lives.

Now, allow me to clarify: Completeness doesn't mean perfection and that everything in life is operating at a level of excellence. Not at all! It just means that a man and a woman have decided to overlook the faults of one another and to sacrifice their time, energy, and effort into seeing that the relationship they desire to build together actually moves to the next level. That's completeness. When the both of you can agree that you want to build, together…that's completeness. When the both of you are willing to try and be understanding of her family issues and his generational tendencies…that's completeness. When the both of you vow to one another to be true, honest, and protective of what you are establishing…that's completeness.

Lily would love to get to that point. As a matter of fact, she has actually moved to that place prematurely only to run the man of her interest away because he wasn't yet at the place of "buy-in." Buy-in signifies that the two of you are able to verbally communicate how you feel, and both of you are ready for a true commitment. Buy-in says that there will be no late night phone calls from other women or from other men and that there are no secrets. Buy-in says that I am willing to make you public knowledge to all that see us so that they will know that you are no longer on the market and that I am willing to secure my investment. That's what buy-in gets you!

But with all the substantial value Lily brings to the table, she is oftentimes still left at the altar of her mind, holding the bouquet, in full wedding regalia, alone in the chapel with the veil pulled over her face to hide the tears of hurt, pain, abandonment, and rejection. Then she must wake from slumber only to find that she is alone and that is her reality.

If I could have a moment to speak to the heart and the mind of Lily, I would say just let go…let go of your past, let go of your pain, let go of your hurt, let go of all of those men who may have wronged you, let go of the bitterness, let go of the hatred, let go of the depression, let go of the internal self judgment and ridicule…LET IT GO! Take their picture down and discard it. Remove their phone number from your cell phone by deleting it. Remove their access to you by cutting off all communication and open opportunities to you. Encourage them to move on with their life so that you may continue on with yours. Celebrate the success of getting them out of your heart, mind, and life. Let them go! As soon as you do this, you will find that there is room in your life for the meaningful things.

I am not saying that it is going to be easy to release them, but I am saying that in order to gain some element of control of your own life and to walk in a realm of peace, you have to let them go. So begin somewhere and begin somehow but begin…NOW! Until you do some cleanup and some throwing out, you will never be ready for the man who is waiting to accept you for who you are. It may not be easy, but you will be amazed at how you may feel once you have allowed the right man in when you have cleaned out the wrong "stuff."

CONSIDERATE

Take a moment to think about the word sacrifice. I will wait. Done? Good. Realistically, when you mention the word sacrifice people begin to think about the giving up of something. Rarely does anyone consider the fact that when you sacrifice, it's supposed to hurt—or at the least, it's supposed to impact your comfort zone. That's where Lily dominates over all of the other Female Types. Lily has mastered the art of sacrifice to the point where she considers others before she even considers herself. She is the type of female who is a forward thinker. She makes every effort to be as understanding and patient as she can because she is used to wanting everyone around her to be happy.

This oftentimes comes at a price for Lily. Some of her friends would use her knowingly because she is considerate and many times she has a hard time saying no. That's a weakness for her. She doesn't say no at work when asked about taking on extra projects that she knows she can't handle. She doesn't say no to the men in her life that she knows add no personal or professional value. She doesn't say no to her family who has made her their scapegoat for everything. It's not her fault that she tries so hard. She has seen other women exploited and used in the same way, but she doesn't know how to just say no for fear of losing the valued relationships around her. See, for Lily, even though she is aware that her employer pushes her around, she finds solace in the fact that she is useful to someone. Even though the men in her midst don't come close to the standard and character of a man whom she would like, that they are paying her any attention at all makes her feel pretty. And as trifling as her family is, she still finds a way to just laugh away the hurt and mockery that she experiences when she is the brunt of their jokes. See, Lily is so considerate that when she is manipulated and taken for granted, she still thinks that because she considers others, there is a hidden barometer and benchmark checklist that gives her points for helping others by denying herself. Sadly, that barometer and benchmark doesn't exist, and Lily fails to see that she can consider others but she must always consider herself in the mix. The side effects of not considering herself are depression, resentment, and anxiety. These types of side effects can produce insomnia, headaches, high blood pressure, and will unsettle your nerves.

Calling out to all the Lilies who may be reading this, get control of your emotions and stop allowing others to use you. Being considerate is a great personality trait to have but not at the expense of your health. Don't just place yourself in a position where you get nothing on your return of investment. Make sure you are vocal to others about what you can do and what you can't do. Be willing to be honest and set boundaries for yourself. Be willing to limit your time out to family and friends and find time to do things that you want to do. Find your "you" time. And don't let anyone take it from you. Continue to be considerate but measure the extent of your consideration in a case-by-case situation. Remember, when you are exhausted at the end of your day and you have no energy left for yourself, that's not consideration…that's abuse. Don't allow others to abuse the consideration you are willing to extend to them.

CHAPTER 4: DAFFODIL

Have you ever tried a new cuisine or fruit drink only to find that it left a bad taste in your mouth? Have you ever had a migraine headache that you just couldn't shake regardless of how much pain medicine you took? Have you ever wished you could have a "do-over" from a decision you made? Men, have you ever known a woman who was so manipulative and cunning that it turned your stomach even to have associated with her? Women, do you know a woman who is controlling, aggressive, cunning, and totally narcissistic? Reader, if you can answer yes to any of the above, then you have undoubtedly met a Daffodil at some point in your life. Sophisticated on some levels and completely urban and backwoods on other levels…that's a Daffodil. She says what you want to hear, only to ignore what you have to say…that's a Daffodil. She is damaged, devious, and degrading…that's a Daffodil. She is a liar—no, not just a liar but a good liar…that's a Daffodil. She will play with your emotions, your manhood, your mind, and your life…that's a Daffodil.

Daffodil is everything that's wrong with women in this world. Daffodil serves as the worst example of a female. Daffodil will devour a Lily and completely fluster and abhor a Tulip. That's because Daffodil is all about herself—at the complete expense of others. She doesn't care what women think about her or what men think about her as long as she is able to survive and sustain her habits.

There is nothing good about a Daffodil other than the fact that she can reproduce. And that alone could prove to be problematic for the world. The reason why a Daffodil is so prevalent is because of one key word…she is damaged! And that damage has transformed her into the controlling, conniving, and critical woman that other women detest and men regret ever knowing.

CONTROLLING

Daffodil is the woman who exemplifies all of the negative stereotypes as it relates to rambunctious women. She can be the Latina woman in the middle of the street with a child on her hips and two at her knee getting ready to fight. She can be the Black woman twisting her neck and waving her finger in the air to prove her point while loud talking everyone else. She can be the Caucasian woman in overalls without any shoes on in the grocery store purchasing a 12 pack of Coors beer. There are a plethora of stereotypes that exist for other cultures and ethnicities that are too numerous to list, but the point is the same…a Daffodil is a Daffodil, is a Daffodil! She will always reveal who she is regardless of how much she tries to hide behind the veil of femininity. She can't help it. She is who she is.

When women see her coming, they try not to whisper expletives under their breath. When men see a Daffodil coming, they try their best to avoid her at all costs. But a Daffodil is cunning. She doesn't need you to participate in her antics, just be a witness to them and a proponent to discussing them later. A Daffodil has to have an audience. That's what makes her thrive. Her power is in putting you on display in a negative way while exalting her ignorance all the while. See, since she is damaged, she now has to be in control of everything and everyone around her. She is unhappy internally and thus wants others to feel the same pain she is feeling, so she makes it her joy to mess with the joy of others. With her controlling angst, she will over talk you, make decisions that negatively impact you, and will run your name and image through the mud.

You may tire in your effort to get through to her because with all of the damage she has encountered in her life, she has built walls of brick and mortar that will require a power drill, a couple of shovels, some wheel barrels, a safety helmet, goggles, gloves, and work boots in order to get through it. You will also need a syringe filled with the most rejuvenating liquid you can find. The syringe will assist in reviving you from fatigue because in breaking down the walls she has erected, it will require stamina, strength, and continued sustenance. That's only if you desire to get to her heart—and she wants to let you in.

One of the most consistent and distinguishable factors of a Daffodil is her controlling spirit. She wants to be the man in the relationship. She wants to be the woman in the relationship. She wants to be the breadwinner in the relationship. She wants to be the one with all the answers in the relationship. She wants to point her finger at you as the reason why things are not working. In all, she does none of the above well. Her controlling nature makes her combative and difficult to communicate with. Her controlling nature makes others stay away from her. Other females won't invite her to social functions and men deal with her at arm's length as they try not to offend her. Daffodil will often use the phrase, "I don't have a lot of female friends because I just don't do well around a lot of women." In essence, what she is saying is that because she is so controlling, other women don't want to be around her because they can't tolerate her foolishness.

Daffodil, hear me…sit down somewhere and realize that you are damaged and you need healing. Destroying the lives of others doesn't help you become whole. Stop being a poison to others and have an enema and clean yourself out to the point where you are not constipated with the garbage of life. Because you are full of garbage, you have an odor, and the more others are around you, the more they pick up your scent. It can't be washed off. You can't cover it with perfume or makeup. You have to deal with it from the inside out. Men, don't let her beauty or her quick tongue distract you from who she really is—a viper. Women, if you value your character and reputation, don't become best friends with a Daffodil unless she is willing to change for the better. Outside of that, avoid her at all costs. The longer you are around her, her controlling nature will ultimately be controlling you.

CONNIVING

It doesn't matter what you say or do, a Daffodil's sole purpose is to get under your skin and infect and affect who you are. She is devious and has an agenda. Regardless of how well you think you can handle her, I mentioned in earlier chapters that she always has a trump card and is skilled at playing it well. Because she is conniving and fearful, she has a way of destroying relationships.

It's amazing how many men are enamored by her even after they realize she would never be marriage material—they just can't leave her alone. But the reality to why men stay around is because she has used her beauty, body, and her brain to ensnare them. And once you are trapped by the 3-B's, you are not the same…ever. When she has you trapped, your mind, heart, and emotions are all messed up. She is very dangerous and unpredictable. You never know what or how she is feeling on any given day. You could have had a great lunch earlier in the day, and when you call her later to check on her, she completely flips on you and you are left wondering what you could possibly have done. She makes statements like, "You don't understand me and as my man, you should know what I expect or want." Another statement could be, "I shouldn't have to say that I want you to come over and spend time with me, it should be a given. We are in a relationship, aren't we?" And yet another statement could be, "I'm just moody today and you should understand." And the biggest one that I know every man has heard before is, "I don't want you to try and fix it. I just want you to listen." But when we listen, you ask us, "Well, do you have a response to what I just told you?"

Some would say that's just women…I would counteract that and say that's just a Daffodil. Most women who are not Daffodils would make an attempt to communicate with their man as to what they may need when they are having a moody moment without making him feel as if he is the cause and root of the situation. Especially when it's his desire to be supportive. Don't turn him away or flip the script on him. But that's a Daffodil, and she will do anything to put the focus on someone else to make them the reason why her life is so convoluted. Daffodil, get a clue! You are conniving and inconsiderate of others. You are selfish, and you need to deal with your issues and stop taking them out on everyone else. Stop whining and casting blame and take ownership of your womanhood. Be an adult for once in your life. The more conniving you become, the more critical you become of others, thereby reducing your level of humanity.

CRITICAL

The last thing that a man needs to hear from a woman is criticism over his efforts to become a better man. When a woman continues to berate a man, he becomes closed off and distant. When a woman compares a man to men of her past, he becomes elusive and will refuse to share. When a woman compares a man to her father, he becomes resentful and he hardens his heart. When a woman expects a man to open up and share his fears with her, and yet she laughs at him when he does, he will then sever his level of commitment to that woman and will seek for it, sometimes unwillingly, in other women.

When a woman is verbally critical of a man, it's like a lightning bolt being slammed through his heart. It is completely emasculating. Well, the lightning bolt award clearly goes to Daffodil. Daffodil has depleted so many men of their masculinity that one can't count the number. Degrading men is something in which she is so well versed that it comes completely natural for her. She doesn't have to ponder when to do it, she does it almost instinctively. She is so skilled in identifying the faults that men possess she has a hard time not commenting on them. Regardless of what image she conveys, she will always reveal her true nature when she opens her mouth.

There are always subtle clues when one encounters a Daffodil, but most men ignore them because of the 3-B's being in effect. For other men, who are a little keener on what they want out of a relationship, they will see the reality of who Daffodil is and they will take off running the other way. They won't return her calls or text messages. They will avoid some of the same local and social places that they both may frequent. They will even come up with an excuse to avoid her if they have to. A critical woman is synonymous with a GPS that keeps reminding you that you have taken a wrong turn on the interstate and there are no exits for another 20 miles…yet the GPS spokesperson will continue to say, "make a u-turn" over, and over, and over. That constant, monotonous voice in our ear telling us the same thing over, and over again is enough to force any man to shut down. Daffodil will constantly remind a man of his worthlessness, of his inferiority, and of his less than manliness standard. Even if he excels in all of those areas, she can find a fault and magnify it to its fullness. Women who are critical of men fail to realize that they do more damage than harm.

Trying to establish a dialogue where the communication can flow from one partner to the next is what one should desire. Any conversation where there is a monologue is not a conversation. Men who have met a Daffodil and who have been degraded by her critical tongue will show visible symptoms. These symptoms include, but are not limited to:

- A guarded heart
- Inability to want to share personal feelings

- An affinity to want to do activities that the woman prefers
- Working overtime
- Avoiding your phone calls by allowing voice mail to pick up
- Rushing you off the phone
- Limiting how often we visit your residence
- Eating out to avoid awkward silences or questions when eating at home
- A high level of frustration
- Potential health problems, including increased blood pressure and headaches

What men and women should desire in order to have healthy relationships is the ability to verbally communicate how they feel, face -to-face—not over the phone or via a text or email. We have to get back to making sure we can hold adult conversations in person while looking at each other eye-to-eye. We have to move from looking for faults in another and begin to expound upon the great value and positive attributes that each can contribute to the relationship. It is not enough to say what we want from another and not offer that or more at the same time. We should not expect from another, what we are not willing to offer of ourselves. If any man encounters a Daffodil, he is unquestionably altered in his emotions and spirit. Any woman who is friends with a Daffodil but who does not have the same traits as a Daffodil can run the risk of becoming a Daffodil.

It's difficult for a Tulip to become a Daffodil because a Tulip is too giving and a Daffodil is concerned with taking and getting. It's easy for a Lily to become a Daffodil if she continues to ignore the things in her past that are keeping her in present day bondage. It's a miracle for a Daffodil to become a Lily, as it requires substantial therapy, intervention, honesty, forgiveness, and a change of behaviors on a daily basis. Changing a Daffodil into a Lily is time consuming and potentially harmful to all involved. See, the Daffodil flower has poisonous secretions within its stem, and if placed in a vase with the Lily flower, the Daffodil will release the poisonous secretions into the water and within three days, the Lily will be dead. By nature, the Daffodil is a survivor at the expense of others.

Daffodil, if after reading this you realize that you want to change and become a Lily, please begin by removing the poisonous secretions in your verbiage that seek to kill off a man. There is a method for your deliverance, but your road to recovery and healing is long. It will be rewarding if you are willing to endure unto the end.

CHAPTER 5: INFECT VS. AFFECT

In my first book, *5 Ways to Affirm a Man*, Chapter 3: Affirmation #2 Communication, I introduce the concept of *"Internal Expectations"* and *"External Realities."* When you are dealing with one of the Male Types (Benin, England, Cuba, or Cyprus), you have to consider your Internal Expectations. In other words, your Internal Expectations are what *you* want to achieve through your communication with your Male Type. Your Internal Expectations are completely controlled by you and you alone. Your External Realities are the responses that may come from the various Male Types as you share your Internal Expectations with them. You have no control at all over the External Realities that may result from what you share with your Male Type. Clearly, men and women communicate in completely different ways. After having scripted that book and after talking with men and women about the concept of Internal Expectations and External Realities, I was asked the following question at a workshop in Oxford, North Carolina: "What happens when a woman doesn't communicate her internal expectations verbally and instead she shows them in her actions?" My reply was, "Then that will totally confuse the Male Type with whom you are dealing."

After some time and after much thought, I came to the conclusion that if a woman is dealing with some internal issues, and they are reflected outwardly, then it's just like having a cold. If your immune system is fighting off a cold internally, then it's reflected outwardly by your actions—puffy and watery eyes, coughing, and lethargy. You don't have to tell someone you have a cold or that you are sick; they can tell by your actions that you are not operating at your full potential. The more you are around others without having fully recovered from your cold, then the greater the chance that you could infect everyone in your entire area by spreading germs. Immediately, the concept of Infect vs. Affect became a subject specifically related to how women perceive, process, and project their feelings and emotions. Let's take a look at each of the impacts that Infect vs. Affect has on Tulip, Lily, and Daffodil.

INFECT

To Have Internal Issues That Reflect Outwardly

When a woman is dealing with her internal emotions, she has a way of either concealing them so that nobody knows or she can be very obvious and allow others to see by her actions that she is troubled. One can tell when a woman is angry, even if she never says a word. When that occurs, you'd better seek an exit door immediately. You may not be the one with whom she is upset, but if you get in her way, you may end up being one of her victims. One can also tell by the way a married woman's skin glows that her husband has been attentive and caring; it radiates from her without her ever having to muster a word—though I am sure she would be more than willing to communicate such a feeling to encourage other women. It's amazing to me to see how a mother can look at her teenage daughter and just know that something is going on with her emotionally and sometimes even physically, much to the daughter's awe.

Some women wear their emotions on their shirtsleeves or across their faces. Other women might require you to perform a surgical procedure in order to find out what is going on with them internally. Yet, at some point, every woman expresses some level of internal sentiment externally without ever having to say what she is feeling. Let's take for instance the Female Types, Tulip, Lily, and Daffodil. Each woman processes her internal emotions in completely different ways. After reviewing each way, consider whether you can relate to them on any level.

TULIP'S INFECT

If you are dealing with a Tulip in your life, you will be the individual who will have the hardest time figuring out what is going on with her internally. Of all the Female Types, she is the one who is most experienced in not displaying what she is feeling. She is so good at not letting on to what is going on with her emotionally that if you didn't already know her and were challenged to guess her age, you would not be able to do it. Tulips don't look their age at all. They have a graceful, time-suspended look. That speaks to her ability to preserve herself so that she is around to help others. Remember, Tulip sees herself as a vital resource for others. Tulip has had to work when her entire body was wracked with pain, and she never told a soul how she was feeling. Tulip has had to endure mental pain and anguish for her family and even her friends and never even uttered a word as to how hurt she really was. Tulip has had things taken away, repossessed, sold off, stolen, stripped away, lost, washed away, forgotten, misused, overused, never used, and even abused, and yet she was able to start over. With all the loss, pressure, strain, pulling, giving, and taking that she has encountered, it has made her resilient, strong, balanced, improved, durable, malleable, and unbreakable! Yet, in her strength lies her weakness.

Because her infect displays as strength to others, the truth is that she is really in need of comfort, understanding, love, and attention. Tulip struggles with how to display that in her actions. Men may determine that she doesn't really need him because she has it all together. That's definitely not the case for this Female Type. She likes for others to think that she has it all together. She likes for others to see her as their never ending resource. She likes to feel needed and in presenting the image and character that she does, it also displays a false message to men. Tulip has even made the statement that she doesn't really need a man. Nothing could be further from the truth. With all that she brings to the table, she lacks the ability to effectively communicate her needs.

To Tulip, being vulnerable denotes an area of insecurity. To appear to others that she may not be able to be a resource would definitely hurt her feelings deeply. The only thing that will allow Tulip to express her internal emotions externally is time and trust. She has to work herself up to the point where she wants to allow another to know where she stands emotionally. She has to trust that once she does so, that individual would not leave her or abandon her. She is used to enduring on her own and with or without a mate to assist her. But once she meets that man who is able to predict and detect what her infect is before she can even share it with him, she will be committed to him for life.

LILY'S INFECT

Lily can't help it! Her feelings are never well hidden. Even when she tries to hide her feelings from others, she doesn't do a very good job of it at all. She gets stressed easily. She becomes disheveled very easily. She gets confused easily. All when she doesn't have control of her internal emotions. Lily's infect will be the most visible of all of the Female Types. She will even try to misdirect others. She will even try to pretend that nothing is wrong with her, but people can tell.

Have you ever had acne appear on your nose overnight? You have no idea where it came from, and it's obvious that it's not going away today. You have a very important business meeting and presentation and you have this huge pimple on your nose. You put some acne fighting cream on it in the hopes that somehow, it will miraculously disappear, but it doesn't. By the time you get to your office, and just before you begin your presentation, you run to the restroom and take one last look at your face—only to find that the pimple has now grown three times larger than what it was initially.

You walk into your meeting, begin your presentation, and do all you can in order to direct attention away from your face. Yet you feel as if everyone in the room is looking directly at you because you are the center of attention. That's how Lily feels ninety-eight percent of the time. She feels that her emotions are continually on display for others to see, and she struggles with being able to conceal them with witty words about alternate subjects not related to her person. She finds ways of engaging others about their life or weekend activities so that she won't have to address the fact that she was let down again by a man who promised one thing and delivered nothing. Many times, Lily will make herself busy so as not to appear depressed, stressed, or distressed. But making yourself busy doesn't change the office talk about you. Making yourself distant doesn't stop family members from conversing about you. Inundating yourself with chores and activities and events doesn't absolve your friends from wondering whether you are having a nervous breakdown.

When any man deals with a Lily who wears her feelings on her sleeves, he will either have to be a very patient man or he will become fed up and walk away from her. Now, it's not that Lily can't discuss what she is feeling or can't verbalize what she may need. The issue is that she may be so volatile that when she begins talking about her internal feelings, she may never stop. She may end up running a man off instead of drawing him nearer. She normally has so much going on all at the same time that she doesn't often have personal time. She tries very hard to appear stable and balanced, but most of the time her internal emotions are on the verge of a breakdown. Many times, she has questioned whether she might be schizophrenic, or at least bipolar. She cries at night to get a break from the problems in her life. She recites her favorite biblical scripture to feel spiritual, even if she isn't. She has a plethora of inspirational quotes and books that she references to lift her emotions from a state of depression. Her journals are many and are filled to completion from cover to cover.

Lily's infect is visible and out there for public judgment. As a woman, she hasn't learned how to compartmentalize the affairs of her life and day. She is great with helping others bring order to chaos, but the chaos in her own life goes unresolved. Unless she begins to put her past issues in their proper perspective, she will be on the verge of a mental breakdown and everyone and everything around her will be affected by it. What may be even more dangerous for her is that, if she doesn't recover and become the Lily that she desires to be, she may end up becoming the Daffodil that nobody ever expected her to be. And that alone means trouble for the rest of the world.

DAFFODIL'S INFECT

By now you should have a very clear understanding and expectation of what a Daffodil's personality and behavior trait can be. You may already be able to predict what you think this segment may entail. But Daffodil is the tricky Female Type. She knows what you may expect of her and sometimes, just for the sheer thrill of it, she may throw you a curve ball. When it comes to her emotions, that's exactly how she intends to play you. Oh no, she won't play herself, but she will definitely play you. See, for Daffodil, she doesn't plan on wearing her feelings on her sleeves, and if for some reason her internal emotions are exposed, she will somehow, some way, flip it on you to make you believe it's all you. It's an amazing tactic and, with what seems to be very little effort, Daffodil can make you second guess yourself or even question your intent and motives when clearly she created the emotional atmosphere in which you find yourself.

Daffodil has what I call the *"atomic element."* Allow me to take you to biology class. An atom is what makes up matter, and matter is what makes up things. An atom is comprised of particles and these particles are known as protons, neutrons, and electrons. Now here is what is interesting about the atom and its parts. Pay close attention. In the very center of the atom are a cluster of protons and neutrons bound together, and this is known as the nucleus (center) of the atom. Floating around the nucleus in an electromagnetic field are electrons, which are negatively charged. In order to determine what type of element exists, it depends upon the quantity of protons, neutrons, and electron particles that reside within the atom.

Now, how does an atomic element relate to the Female Type, Daffodil? Glad you asked that question. Daffodil is known for being the nucleus or the center of attention. Even with all of the positive elements and people floating around in her vicinity, she still can manage to produce an electromagnetic field of electrons that will emit negativity to all who encounter her. Daffodil has a way of turning a great family gathering into a family feud (and I don't mean the game show from the 80's) all because of her negativity. She has been known to bring division between her girlfriends because of something negative that she has said or because she has misapplied a truth. She seems to generate an energy that forces people to dislike her and to dislike being around her. And all of this is part of her infect!

She is well aware that she can be negative and that others know that about her also. She strategically uses her emotions to corral the negative energy out to others at a very low level, all the while completely dismissing any care or concern about the repercussions that may come about because of her behavior. Yes, she is smart, cunning, and strategic. But if challenged in front of others, she will sometimes lose her self-control and resort to being the loud, brash, rude, and verbally attacking woman who is completely absent decorum or candor. She unleashes the beast within.

Unless you are willing to go toe-to-toe with her all the way, I would suggest you choose your weapons and tactics carefully. Sometimes walking away and avoiding the onslaught of her attacks may be your smartest and safest move ever. Not to worry, there will be many other opportunities to deal with her on your own turf, but today may not be that day. Beware of the atomic element of a Daffodil. Her negativity is infectious and can spread very rapidly. Be careful how close you get to her and how close you allow her to get to you. Remember, you can see a cloud of negativity from far off, and it can linger for some time before dissipating. The type of impact it can have on you depends upon how long you allow yourself to be under it.

AFFECT

To Have External Reflections Based Upon External Situations

Every Female Type is responsive to "affect." The two topping the list are Tulip and Daffodil. To have external reflections based upon external situations simply means that whatever is happening around an individual, they are reactive to it. Their reaction is directly related to what the external situation may be. The reaction is not based on something from the past; it's a present day reaction triggered entirely by the external situation that has occurred.

An example of an external reflection based upon an external situation is when an individual witnesses a car accident occurring during a snowstorm and there is nothing at all that they could have done to prevent it from occurring. They witness it happening in real time and are helpless to do anything about it.

Another example would be to come home early from work unannounced and to walk in on your underage teenager and two of her high school friends drinking alcoholic beverages under your roof. There may be many emotions that you may have at the time but you must now react to what the external situation has presented you. There is nothing you could have done to prevent that from happening because it was outside of your control.

That's what makes this particular segment so pivotal…you can't control the action, only your reaction. And that is where the problem may lie for all of the

Female Types. You can think about what you would have done before the external situation presented itself. You can reflect on what your parents or friends may have done if in the same situation, but the reality is, you don't know what you would do until you have been placed in a given situation. And this is where the external reflection becomes your reality in the present realm. This is the only segment in this entire book where the Female Types all have something in common. They will all react to the external situation. They will all show emotion in their reactions. But they won't all experience the same results from their reactions. Let's explore this in detail.

TULIP'S AFFECT

Tulip is the passionate, reactionary type of female. She is going to get involved, try to help, and offer her services because she is reactionary by nature. If there is a car accident, she is going to pull over and try and assist, or she will be the one who is on her cell phone calling the police to report the accident. If there is a physical altercation in her vicinity, she is going to take steps to stop it, and she may even run over and physically try to break it up without regard for her own safety. If there is a tragedy or death that has occurred, she will be sure to send a sympathy card or even offer condolences—even if she wasn't close to the individual or the family that's grieving. She will reflect on it after she has already engaged herself in the situation.

Now, when it comes to her man, she is very protective and defensive of him. He could have been gone from the house for three nights straight, and she will still speak good things about him and protect his character. See, Tulip has a unspoken understanding with her man. He knows she is there and isn't going anywhere, and he knows that as long as he comes home, calls, expresses some element of concern, it will be fine with Tulip at least for a little while. See, Tulip will give her man a lot of rope to do what he wants to do. The problem with doing this is that she tends to put up with more mess than the average woman would. But that's Tulip. In her mind, it's easier to deal with who she has and what she is getting than to try and start all over again with someone new.

Tulip could live a much happier and fulfilled life, but she is willing to allow those pleasantries to bypass her because she lives in the present. In her mind, some of the things that she sees other women running after or even striving for are beyond her sphere. She is content where she is and with what she has. She is fully reflective that it should be different…that it could be different, but what about right now? She wants to make right now work for her and her man. Right now matters to Tulip and for her, her external reflections have to be based upon her current external situations. Today matters and tomorrow will take care of itself.

LILY'S AFFECT

Lily is the passive, passive reactionary type of female. If she were to witness a theft occurring in a department store, she would probably not report it, and she would probably not confront the individual. She would look around to see if others are aware, and she would immediately become concerned for her welfare and safety. Some of her external reflections would be to consider leaving the store immediately for fear of what may happen if she stays. Another reflection she may have is to go to another level or floor within the same store so that she is removed from the situation totally.

If Lily were to become aware that her manager or a colleague is stealing from the company or forging documents illegally, she would never confront them or even bring it up. She would ensure that her documents were legitimate and that she can account for her time and work ethic accordingly.

If she is with a man that is cheating on her and she finds out, she won't immediately call him on it or end the relationship. She will wait with the expectation that it may become better or he may leave his mistress alone entirely. She will suppress her emotions and fake her way through the hurt she feels. But the emotions will stay on her mind and in her heart, sometimes for months and even years after the event has occurred.

She has always desired to be happy and safe and secure and wanted and loved and provided for and to know that she has value…but many if not all of those wants tend to elude her daily, weekly, monthly, yearly. And so she suppresses her anger. She suppresses her hurt. She suppresses her rage. And she denies her reality and adds layer upon layer upon layer of regret…of un-fulfillment…of sacrifice…of rejection. See, Lily doesn't do well to responding to her external situations. She would rather not have a response and make herself numb to it than to have to fight her way through her external reflections. She doesn't like to fight. It takes so much of her energy to fight for what she believes in.

She had better learn to fight. If not, she will end up destroying herself because of the internal combustion that may occur from emotional repression. She has to find a way of coping and releasing all of that backed up tension that's in her neck and in her hands and in her legs and in her chest and in her back and don't let me forget to mention the knots in her stomach. Lily's reflections normally leave her in shambles. She will sleep it off and awake to a new day with new challenges and new reflections, and the previous night's stresses will just get layered on.

Lilly has what I would label as the *"compound effect."* She is the only Female Type who has more emotional baggage than she knows what to do with. The compound effect simply states that she will continue to layer her problems instead of dealing with them. She is so congested with past issues that her breathing and endurance has been impacted by it. She is literally making herself sick because she is so weighed down by her issues. Hopefully, she will be able to meet the man of her dreams who will be strong, in focus, and yet gentle in his handling of her emotions. That's what she will drift off to sleep thinking as she continues to wipe away the tears of her past, which have crippled her present.

Rest tonight, Lily, and dream of what could be as tomorrow prepares to greet you bright and early with its new trials.

DAFFODIL'S AFFECT

Daffodil's affect is always laced with her opinion of the situation. She is almost always going to put herself in the situation even if it has nothing to do with her. If she witnesses a boyfriend and girlfriend arguing in public, she is going to render her opinion of the situation even if it's to a total stranger. She is going to be loud and unsympathetic about it. But that's Daffodil. If she sees a mother with her child at the park and the child is refusing to obey the mother, Daffodil is the type who would try and correct the mother for not being more stern or direct with her child. And what's funny about the situation is Daffodil may not even have any children, but she is still going to react to the external situation that's before her.

When it comes to men, Daffodil is known for leaving him feeling embarrassed and belittled. She will make personal attacks publicly just because she can. She is the type of woman who will follow you through the streets, arguing to prove her point as you try and walk away and leave the situation alone. She is the type who will want to grab you by your shirt and put her finger in your chest to prove her point. And she could care less as to who is watching while she is performing. That's what Daffodil truly enjoys…performing for her audience. If she doesn't have an audience, she will still perform, but when she has a captive audience, she goes in for the encore presentation.

What's disheartening about Daffodil is that she could have made her point without the ostentatious showmanship. It's not that Daffodil doesn't know how to communicate with a level of self-control and discretion; it's that she loses control and before she knows it, it's too late. She may apologize at a later date, but by then the verbal assault and damage have already taken place.

Men, may I remind you, Daffodil is normally a product of her environment and that may not be a good thing at all. She doesn't want to be tamed and doesn't like to be told what to do. She likes control, freedom, and living life without restraints. But you know as well as I do the reason why automobiles have seatbelts—for your protection. Restraints are in place to provide you with a sense of security and protection. Isn't it interesting how Daffodil is the only female type who sees restraints as a negative thing?

Women, being free-spirited is not a bad thing necessarily, but having no care for how you present yourself to others and completely ignoring the feelings of others is a dangerous position in which to place yourself. Learn from the examples that I have provided for you. If you are a Daffodil and you are reading this book and you have an attitude, good! Why wouldn't you? You are only reacting to the external situation that reading this book has placed you in. You are only proving that my analysis of you is accurate. Now instead of getting angry, allow me to provide you with the option of seriously taking an introspective look at yourself and how you are perceived. If you know that you fit the characteristics mentioned throughout this book, seek ways to change and improve. Look for that one friend who will tell you how it really is and allow them to help you become a better woman.

For most Daffodils, therapy and relocation are great remedies for you. Seek all the therapy you need so that you can have a neutral individual who will help you get over you! You can't continue to blame others for being the way that you are. Decide today that you would like to improve and then begin making small improvements in your character, in your communication, and in your composure. Take your castor oil with a spoon full of sugar and deal with your issues. Stop making everyone else sick…sick of you and sick with you!

CHAPTER 6: LEARNING STYLES

VISUAL, AUDITORY & KINESTHETIC/TACTILE

There are a plethora of resource materials online, at bookstores, and located at every library and institution of higher learning that relate to the "learning styles" of individuals. So much has been studied and written about them, and they have even been incorporated into business models as companies seek to hire employees. Please take the time to research the specifics of each at your leisure. Yet, I would be remiss if I didn't mention at least a few of the well known or most discussed learning styles. By no means is the following a complete list, but it is very important to identify with one or more of the learning styles as it relates to who you are as a female and how you relate to others.

In society, we have a tendency to make things race based, gender based, age based, or economic based. I would implore you to look at life, people, circumstances, and situations on a completely higher level…look at life through observation, information, and application and how those three concepts affect our behaviors and our perceptions. I will expound more on this throughout this chapter, but let's get you the basis of the learning styles because you will need that as we begin to increase our cognition (how we think about thinking) in this chapter.

As I begin to discuss the learning styles, please note that not all women are alike and not all men are alike. We group them in categories because it makes it simple (or so we would like to think) for us as a people to relate to women, or men, or race, or gender, or age. But I have learned that simply categorizing individuals happens because we are sometimes afraid to reveal how closely we may identify with them on certain levels.

LEARNING STYLES

While pursuing my bachelor's degree from Norfolk State University, I heard of a professor who was very well known throughout the entire university for being able to recall material on each page and each chapter of a book without ever looking at the book during his lectures. Prior to taking his class, I was informed by many students that this professor was difficult, strict, assigned a huge load of homework, and he did not accept work late…at all. I was also informed, and it was documented, that he and Malcolm X had debated each other. Imagine that! I was actually going to meet an individual who had been in a debate with Malcolm X. I was fascinated and drawn to find out more about this professor, who so many tried to avoid. Many students detested taking any classes from him, but in order to graduate, you had to take two courses that were taught by him. So unless you transferred out of the university, there was no way to avoid taking his class.

My very first class and semester with him is when I learned how to build, strengthen, and even broaden my learning style skill set. It was in his class that I learned that I was a true auditory learner. The course was Critical Thinking, and I had never been challenged to such a degree intellectually as I had with this professor. He forced me to think about everything and not just accept things at face value. He forced me to be able to research any position that I choose in life and to support it with factual data in order to defend it. He taught me to remember time, dates, events, people, and results. It was amazing. During this class, we reviewed the learning styles of individuals: visual learners, auditory learners, and kinesthetic/tactile learners.

Visual Learners

Visual learners are those individuals who can see it done once or twice and then they can duplicate the task. They are the individuals who can see a picture of how something is to look when completed by simply looking at the box and then performing the tasks to get to that result. They are imaginative thinkers and are not necessarily good with time or following a step-by-step procedure. Visual learners bore easily, like to work at their own pace, and normally have a completely different roadmap to accomplishing a task. They may take a special interest in puzzles, mazes, building things, and in seeing patterns that others may miss. They are great at what they see but may have issues in what they hear (remember). This leads us to the second type of learner to be discussed, auditory learners.

Auditory Learners

Auditory learners are those who learn best by hearing information and not just by visualizing it. I learned that I can sit in an auditorium with over 200 students and be able to listen to the professor give his lecture and still be able to recollect everything that was said while taking copious notes. While others were on their cell phones, or sleeping, or doing class work for other professors, I was tuned in and focused on what it was that I should be learning from the professor at the podium. It was great.

Auditory learners have the keen ability to remember details, dates, events, and data quite accurately. They are attracted to word games, have an increased vocabulary level, and are engaged in reading and researching multiple topics that may or may not be related to each other. Oftentimes, auditory learners are great conversationalists because they learn a little about a lot of topics. More often than not, an auditory learner who has taken the time to develop their skillset will prove to be a pretty good listener and a relatively good communicator. They normally have a keen sense of rhythm and are drawn to musical interests, be it singing or playing an instrument. They enjoy reading out loud, are not afraid to engage others in dialogue, enjoy working on team-centered activities, and are not good with being still or quiet for long periods of time. They do exceptionally well with writing essays and responses to a lecture but not so well with a timed test, as it restricts their thinking process. This type of learning style is completely opposite that of the kinesthetic/tactile learner, who learns by doing and experiencing life.

Kinesthetic/Tactile Learners

Kinesthetic/Tactile learners are those who have to be a part of what it is they are learning. In other words, they need to be able to touch, experience, and participate with life in order to fully grasp and have an understanding of what it is they are learning. Of all the learners, they will be the most bored if they had to listen to a prolonged lecture or sit through a meeting that lasts more than thirty minutes. Their particular learning style is best enhanced when they are physically part of the learning. Kinesthetic/tactile learners are individuals who may gravitate toward any of the following professions: seamstress/tailor, mechanic, chef/baker, artist/painter, an athlete, scientist, or anything physical such as dance, traveling, building things with their hands, or martial arts.

On tests or exams, they do better with multiple choice or fill-in-the-blanks. They don't do so well with extensive tests, essays, or even with having to come up with ideas on the spur of the moment. Kinesthetic learners are the type of individuals who can study while the television and radio are all on at the same time.

Every woman fits into one of the three aforementioned learning styles, and some women have no clue that their learning style affects their behavioral responses as it relates to men and others. Each of the female types in this book possesses a primary learning style that is directly connected to their behavioral responses and how they learn and filter information. Pay close attention to how each female type is described as it relates to their observation of situations, application of what they experience, and informational responses to those experiences.

If I were to assign a learning style to each of the female types, it might look something like the following grid:

FEMALE TYPE	LEARNING STYLE
Tulip	Kinesthetic/Tactile
Lily	Visual
Daffodil	Auditory

Further exploration and clarity will be provided as you continue to read.

OBSERVATION

"BASED UPON WHAT HAPPENS TO OTHERS"

Observation is our ability to assess life based on what happens to others. Normally, when we observe things, we make a determination about that situation and our responses vicariously. Simply put, when we observe others, we make a judgment call about them and about ourselves. It can be a positive observation or it can be a negative observation, but the end result is that we are affected either positively or negatively by what someone else has gone through or experienced…even though we may have nothing at all to do with what they may have encountered.

For example, when we hear about close friends who may be going through a difficult time in their marriage, observation forces us to look at our own marriage and question it or celebrate it all the more. We may be inclined to take sides or choose who we are willing to support or no longer support based upon what we know or what we have seen. When we hear about a neighbor's teenage daughter becoming pregnant before completing high school, it makes us question the actions of our own child and what they may be participating in without our knowledge. We may decide to have a very serious talk with them at that time about life and the consequences of the decisions they make. All triggered by what has been observed about someone else's child.

Observation makes one aware of circumstances and that, in turn, forces us to change our behaviors. Whereas observation is visual, information is mental. Information is what we are directly exposed to. It's not just visual but it's also relational. With information, we are required to do something with it. It's not abstract. It has a direct correlation to our life.

INFORMATION

"WHAT WE ARE EXPOSED TO"

Information is what we are directly exposed to. It is not vicarious and abstract. It has to be related to something we know, have heard, and can validate, or it's related to something we were a part of or that we triggered to happen.

When I was a young child, around the age of ten years old, I used to steal money out of my mother's purse. We lived in a huge house in Connecticut that had a basement. I would steal three or four dollars out of my mother's purse and then would run to the corner store along with two of my friends from the neighborhood. We would purchase chips, soda, and candy and then would sneak to the basement to devour it without my mother ever knowing the money was missing. I was sure I'd mastered the art of thievery because I was able to get away with it at least four or five times without ever getting caught.

It wasn't until one day I was informed that our lights were going to be turned off due to lack of payment on the bill. Now I had no idea how we had gotten to that point, but the reality is the bill came, my mother called to get an extension and was denied, and the information she shared with me that day directly affected my profession of thievery. I began to feel bad about all those times that I had stolen from her. I realized that I was a contributor to the fact that our lights were going to be turned off. In my mind, as a child, had I not taken the money so often, maybe, somehow, the money would have been enough to pay the bill and my mother would not have to be worried about having our lights disconnected.

As an adult, I know that there was no way that the little bit of money I had taken could have resolved that situation, but as a child, the information given altered my behavior at that time. I stopped stealing that day. Though that's a very simplistic and even humorous example, the point is still the same. The information that you receive and are exposed to has a direct impact on your behavior and responses. You could have been exposed to information that relates to your marriage or your family, and it has you contemplating how you are going to navigate through your day. You may have been exposed to information about layoffs or corporate downsizing events that may be happening at your place of employment. This will definitely have a direct impact on how you will manage your finances and career over the next couple of weeks or months. You could have been exposed to information about your child. It's the kind of thing that keeps you up at night and distracted during the day. What are you going to do?

Observation is what we observe about others, but information is what directly affects us individually. Either way, some decisions have to be made. But true learning comes from the application of what you have observed and been exposed to (information). Trial and error is the true sign of growth and maturity. Until you mess up a few times, you will never learn from certain things.

APPLICATION

"TRIAL AND ERROR"

The application of anything is based upon your observation (scope), your information (what you know), and the application (trial and error) of all three. My son had a science project wherein his instructor asked the entire class, "Have you ever seen a bottle of Coca-Cola explode?" The kids in his class were excited (as all kids in the 8th grade would be to see a science project explode). Many kids were doubtful that it could happen because they had never seen it occur (observation). Others were doubtful even though they were getting their information directly from the professional (the instructor), and they were completely in disbelief. Others were excited to be a part of the process.

The students had to have certain elements in place in order for the experiment to work. They needed one liter of Coca-Cola, four individual pieces of Mentos candies, and a 6-inch tubular cylinder with a screw top cap. Some of the students were provided with cold liters of Coca-Cola and others were provided with warm liters of Coca-Cola. All the students were provided with the exact same instructions. They had to remove the cap from the one-liter Coca-Cola container, drop the four Mentos candies into the container, attach the 6-inch tubular cylinder with the screw top cap to the Coca-Cola container, and then shake it up vigorously.

The group of students who had the cold containers of Coca-Cola saw the Mentos candies float to the top of the container and dissipate…no explosion of the Coca-Cola occurred. The other group of students who had the warm containers of Coca-Cola saw a completely different reaction. They performed the exact same procedure, but once the Mentos candies floated to the top of the container, the soda began to fizz rapidly and the explosion occurred.

The only thing different about each experiment was the "temperature" of the soda in each container. And this is where we draw our correlation to the female types. Based upon the learning styles of the female types and their internal temperature at the time, they will have a completely different behavioral response to you and even within themselves.

FEMALE TYPES AND THEIR LEARNING STYLES

Based upon the knowledge that I have already provided to you about each female type and about the learning styles of individuals, you will find that the female types actually exemplify a certain type of learning style that can be associated with their behavioral responses. All of this observation, coupled with information and then applied accordingly, could create a different type of behavior if the "elements" are mixed correctly and the internal temperature of the female type is legitimate (please refer back to the science project). Everything depends upon the internal temperature of the female type, which will determine your end result as you interact with them. The grid below will serve as a barometer as you read through this section.

FEMALE TYPE	LEARNING STYLE	INTERNAL TEMPERATURE
Tulip	Kinesthetic/Tactile	Warm
Lily	Visual	Cold
Daffodil	Auditory	Hot

Tulip's Learning Style

Most female types that resemble Tulip are patient, understanding, have fewer hang-ups and issues, and are more forgiving than the other female types. Tulips are kinesthetic/tactile by nature because they have to be involved and engaged in the situation at hand. They are not merely observers or merely well informed; they methodically apply what they have observed and are informed about when it comes to men. Tulips are the type of women who are normally warm internally because they will have a response or a reaction, but it may not be the one you are looking for or would expect. If they are bothered by something that a man does, they will react, but it may not be a "blow up," per-se. Their behavioral response could be to pull back and not share as easily if their pride or person were offended. They will let you know, but it may be in the form of a quick-witted comment or sharp verbal retort. It would rarely be in the form of throwing things or breaking things, or cursing, or being physically violent. But there will always, and I repeat, there will always be some type of behavioral change when this female type is negatively or positively affected. But rest assured, it would rarely be a blow-up.

Most men who are more consumed with themselves than with their mate would completely overlook and not even be sensitive to the behavioral changes that may occur in Tulip. Most of the behavioral changes that will occur in this female type are mostly related to her internal response. Tulips can handle the conflict that may come because of a given situation, but they will most always approach it with a level head and not out of emotional instability. One of the reasons they enjoy being alone is because it gives them time to rehearse, formulate, and determine what they will do when the opportunity presents itself. They can deal with a lot because they have mastered the art of "chunking it up." They can put things they are dealing with in their internal compartment and "shelve" it for another time. They are great at not allowing the pressures and stresses of life to overwhelm them all at once. Chunking it helps them to deal with issues in staggered time frames and in small portions. They have mastered this craft, and no other female type comes close to even matching this skill that Tulip possesses. Tulip has a greater tendency to move her internal temperature from "warm" to "cold" but rarely from "warm" to "hot."

Lily's Learning Style

The visual learning style best fits this female type. She definitely has to see it to believe it, and she has heard all the talk before. She is interested in something real...something tangible. She has to be able to see it because she knows how she wants to feel, but she is tired of hearing all the jargon from men that goes with what a relationship should consist of. She has heard the verbiage associated with the game and she is tired of it. She has seen you play her, her friend, and her cousin, and she is done with it. She doesn't want you to talk her to death, but proof is in the pudding for her. She must and has to see it visibly walked out before her in order for her to respond accordingly. Unlike Tulip, you won't see an immediate behavioral response from Lily. She will sometimes allow you to see what you want to see, but that's not always the reality of who she is or of how she feels.

Lily's internal temperature is cold. That means, it takes a long time before she explodes. She is the type of female who has been so mentally and in several instances, emotionally and physically abused by men that she has completely shut off her emotions and will only allow you to see what she wants you to see. Of all the female types, she is in the most non-responsive state. It's much harder to predict what she will do because she can adapt to environments well while camouflaging how she really feels. She would like for your words to be potent and impactful, but she has heard the same lines so many times from so many different men that she is just turned off. She would rather internally torment herself than let a man get close to her heart.

But here is the interesting scenario in which Lily finds herself. She wants a man to be able to earn and win her heart, but she has a fear of being totally vulnerable and transparent—even though that's what she ultimately desires. She is a believer and supporter of love. She is a romantic to the best of her abilities. She is also an emotional wreck, and until a man can take the time to invest in her and wait on the return, she will continue to be the least responsive female type. It is amazing how she can gauge the emotions of others, offer encouraging words and direction, and yet, she is as closed off and disconnected from the rest of her emotions as a bank vault.

One would prefer that Lily move her internal temperature from "cold" to "warm," but it takes time and sacrifice. Lily would love to be warm and reactionary, but life has hardened her and stolen her joy. She must fight to regain it if she desires to be truly respected for the woman that she can become…not for the woman she currently is.

Daffodil's Learning Style

It should by no means come as a surprise that Daffodil's learning style is auditory and that her internal temperature is "hot." Daffodil is bossy, temperamental, controlling, argumentative, and impatient. She wants what she wants, when she wants it. She is auditory because she listens for the flaws in what you may say or do so that she can use them against you. She is verbal in her responses and frequently "explodes"—sometimes at the most inopportune times and places. She is embarrassing at family events, in the mall, at the grocery store, or even in the community park. If you are a man and you are dealing with a Daffodil, you will find yourself continually trying to maintain her internal temperature between cold and warm. If it begins to intensify to "hot," you may want to remove yourself to a more neutral and controlled environment.

Daffodil's behavioral response is always predicated upon what is going on with her internal temperature. Daffodil's are not good with remembering everything they hear, but they are great at connecting things together from what they may have heard or experienced. Sometimes they connect things that have no correlation to what may be going on currently, but they have an uncanny way of making things fit that don't fit and then reversing those same things to use against you in an attacking manner. It's amazing how they can vacillate between being calm one moment and then completely unreasonable the next moment.

There are key distinguishable traits that every Daffodil possesses: their behavioral responses are always predicated upon what is happening within them internally. They will always verbalize their response to a situation (even if it doesn't involve them), and they are very attacking (verbally), to the point of being insulting. They only see things in their perspective when they are in a full, heated discussion. More than likely, you will not be able to get your point across until after they have had some time to calm down and reflect on how things went. Even then, their behavior may not change immediately.

Men, after reading this book, you should be able to spot a Daffodil from across the room. You will need to determine whether it is your intention to engage her even before she shows you her real personality. Remember, a Daffodil is clever. She can dress the way you want her to dress; she can respond the way you want her to respond; and she can even react the way she thinks you would want her to react—but all of these are temporal. She is not as well skilled as Lily is at masking what she is feeling. Sometimes, a little disagreement will push Daffodil over the edge of exposing her true sentiment. She is not as controlled and polished with her emotions as a Tulip.

Daffodil doesn't have the endurance of time and testing to reflect that type of self-control. Daffodil will bring you trouble, stress, high blood pressure, migraine headaches, and even gray hair. Daffodil can cause you to leave your family, ignore your children, and disconnect from your friends and even your social activities. Every woman has the power of persuasion, but none more so than Daffodil. If she sees something that she wants, she is going to go after it—even if that means stepping on and hurting others along the way. Most men would not want to deal with a Daffodil. But there are some who are under the auspices that they can change her and conquer her. Those men are few and far between. And those same men are the ones you see being controlled, yelled at, and led around like a child in public. I am sure we can all identify with knowing at least one Daffodil and that we can feel empathy for the men in their lives. Remember, it's a choice. You can choose to be with Tulip, Lily, or Daffodil, but all of your choices have consequences. It's up to you to determine what you are willing to endure.

Men, I would say avoid a Daffodil altogether. But if you are the adventurous type and feel compelled to explore her, be sure you have a great support network that she doesn't know about. That may be the only way you will be rehabilitated from the war wounds you are inevitably going to receive.

CHAPTER 7: RECOVERY

Anyone who knows me personally knows that I have never desired to be a psychologist or a sociologist or a biologist or anything of the sort. Those who know me personally would say that I am a deep thinker, that I enjoy lively and controversial dialogue, and that the only real way to deal with any situation or emotion is through communication. Those who know me personally trust my wisdom, allow space for me idiosyncrasies, and realize that I can be emotional, distant, compelling, sensitive, and difficult at times. And yet, without question, anyone who knows me personally will attest to the fact that I try with all my heart to be fair, honest, and inclusive. I can be forgiving, fun, and even silly, but I am always aware, learning, and applying ideas, concepts, precepts, and experiences in order to make my life better.

Learning never stops. In other words, the recovery process is never stagnant or idle…it's always in motion, as energy is. I have recovered from a Daffodil (or two or three…lol), and I have used a Tulip to assist me in growing up. I have lost a Lily, never to regain her again. I have experienced the Female Types, and they have helped me to understand women all the more.

Recovery says that your experience didn't kill you. It may have crippled you, but you can get rehabilitation for what you need, and you can walk again…live again…believe in love again…breathe again…and be a better you…AGAIN! The interesting thing about recovery is that the majority of the belief and strength that you need in order to overcome your situation is already inside of you…it's innate! And isn't it great to be able to experience your recovery process and allow all of those who had counted you out, see you triumphant and alive again? All of those who didn't believe in you…all of those who created false allegations against you for their own personal gains…all of those who made you look like you were at fault, will find with time, their lies and accusations didn't stop your momentum. Make today the day that you begin to **Live Life With No Regrets!**

MY FINAL THOUGHTS

What do I regret most about this piece of work?

I regret the fact that I couldn't use every single response or scenario that women provided to me when I was composing this work. There are many women who have either heard me present on the topic of "Female Types," or they have read a comment that I may have shared, and they have been very honest and candid with me about where they are, who they are, and who it is that they would like to become. Women are always competing with men. They are competing for respect, they are competing for equal salaries, they are competing for similar professional careers, and they are competing for balance in their personal, spiritual, and physical realms. Women are always competing for what they feel rightfully belongs to them, though they may have been looked over or passed over or walked over by men who are less skilled, less qualified, less professional, and who are far more immature.

To all of the women out there who do not see themselves as a Tulip, Lily, or Daffodil—just know that you still have a Female Type and that "type of a female" will always have influence and the ability to impact the male species. The question for you to consider is do you know what your Female Type is, and what impact are you leaving on those whom you may encounter?

What am I most proud of about this piece of work?

I am most proud of the mental and emotional growth that I have experienced because of the work and the exposure to new ideas that this work has afforded me. Women supplied me with information I would never have been able to come up with on my own. I appreciate those women who were not afraid to allow me to enter their mind, heart, home, and their private thoughts in order to be able to help the world with the three Female Types that I created: Tulip, Lily, and Daffodil. If it were not for the Tulips, Lilies, and Daffodils, whom I have encountered in my own life, along with the openness of other women whom I have met, this book would not have been possible.

I am proud of all the women in this world who have been hurt, betrayed, disrespected, and abandoned by men, and yet they still pressed through the hurt. They forgave the betrayal. They encouraged themselves and found their internal efficacy and self-respect, which was always innate. I applaud those women who have not used the dismal times of their lives to take their humanity and their dignity and their power. I applaud Tulips who have realized they can't and don't want to be a second mother to a man. I applaud Lilies who realize they can't live in a depressed state for the remainder of their natural lives, but instead realize that they have value and they can rise above their past and not allow it to control their future. I definitely applaud every Daffodil who is not afraid to say that they are indeed a Daffodil, but that they are seeking support, help, encouragement, and balance to heal and become whole again. I applaud Daffodils who are restoring the men whom they have hurt and even betrayed. Healing begins with forgiving yourself. Recovery begins with asking for forgiveness from those you have hurt.

What have I learned from working on this piece of work?

I have learned that just because a woman says that she can't be put in a "category" or be cast as a "type"—she really can be. Every woman wants to be acknowledged for something she has done or for some impact she has had. It begins even as a child who desires the attention of his or her parents, siblings, teachers, teammates, or friends. Women desire to be recognized—even if it's for the wrong thing. Some recognition is at least recognition.

I have learned that women are great at manipulating situations to their advantage. I have learned that women are great at masking their true feelings. I have learned that women are so forgiving…so understanding…so supportive…so sacrificial…so loving and yet they can be so misunderstood. I have learned to ask questions and wait on the answers. I have learned that the answers may not come immediately, though I may want them to. I have learned that sometimes no answer is still an answer, and that I must realize it's the reality of that situation at that given time. I have learned to be slow to anger, quick to listen, and even quicker to forgive.

I have learned that some women make it very difficult for other women. I have learned that good women can become really bad women without proper balance and without reality checks. I have learned that really evil women find it hard to become less evil women, so most of them stop trying and end up damaging the lives of everyone around them because of this. I have learned that men desire the attention of women, be it intimate or platonic. The desire is still innate.

I have learned that there are many, many, many men who wish they had the opportunity for a "do-over." Men who wish they could go back in time some five years, ten years, and twenty years back and fix, rectify, soften, or even change the things they did incorrectly. There are many men who are hurting, damaged, broken or who have been destroyed by the antics of a woman. Many men and women need to repent, forgive, be restored, and move on with their lives. I would surmise, now is the time. Be the initiator of the change that you desire to see happen in your life. Stop dreaming and wishing that it would occur…be your own catalyst for change. I DARE YOU!

What should you learn after reading this piece of work?

You should have learned that you know a Tulip, Lily, and a Daffodil. You probably know several or all of them, or you may even be living vicariously through one of the Female Types right now. You should have learned that you have influence, and that influence has had an impact on a male somewhere. You should have learned that it's not always the man who can be blamed for why you are the way that you are. You have some responsibility for your actions and your reactions.

Men, you should have learned that you need to mature and grow up in some areas. You need to make better and wiser decisions on the "type" of woman or women that you allow to be a part of your life. You also need to be mature in how you handle situations that are outside of your control. If you meet a Daffodil and you like her image but you despise her character…move on to the next one. Be smarter so you won't end up broken, bitter, and betrayed by your own emotions because you were in denial.

One final thing you should have learned from this piece of work is that we are all still learning how to be better at being the person we are. It takes time, but don't waste your time…use it to your full advantage!

Notes

1. The American Heritage Dictionary. 2nd ed. Boston, MA: Houghton Mifflin Company, 1985.

2. Ibid.

3. Ibid.

4. Ibid.

www.ingramcontent.com/pod-product-compliance
Ingram Content Group UK Ltd.
Pitfield, Milton Keynes, MK11 3LW, UK
UKHW040559210726
13854UKWH00008B/1579

9 781365 763892